Design: Jill Coote
Recipe Photography: Peter Barry
Recipe styling: Jacqueline Bellefontaine, Helen
Burdett, Bridgeen Deery and Wendy Devenish
Jacket and Illustration Artwork: Jane Winton,
courtesy of Bernard Thornton Artists, London
Editorial: Laura Potts

CLB 3356
Published by Grange Books,
an imprint of Grange Books PLC,
The Grange, Grange Yard, London, SE1 3AG
© 1993 CLB Publishing,
Godalming, Surrey, England.
Printed and bound in Singapore
This edition reprinted in 1994
ISBN 1-85627-319-9

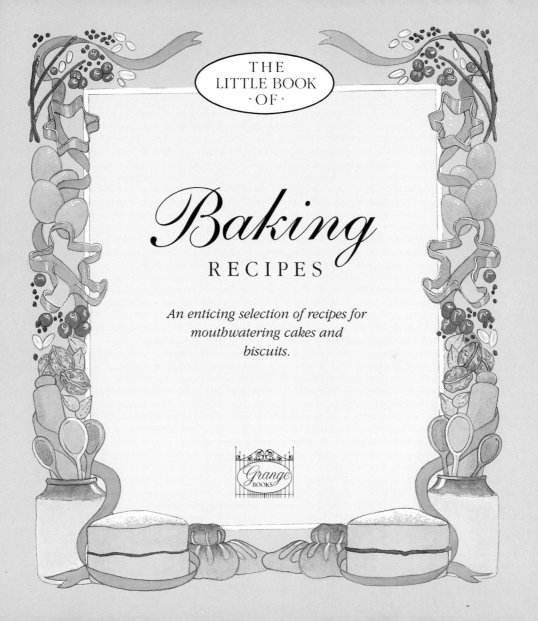

THE
LITTLE BOOK
· OF ·

Baking

RECIPES

An enticing selection of recipes for
mouthwatering cakes and
biscuits.

Grange
BOOKS

Introduction

Walking into a kitchen and being greeted by the smell of freshly baked cake is enough to unlock a flood of childhood memories. It evokes memories of returning home from school to a house filled with tantalizing smells of baking, of teas in front of the fire on cold winter days, and of eating scones filled with strawberries and cream during the hot, lazy days of summer. Most importantly; people remember the sense of mystery that they felt as a child as they watched sugar and butter being creamed, as eggs were separated and beaten, and as the last of carefully weighed ingredients were incorporated into the mixture.

In days gone by recipes were passed from generation to generation, though frequently they were not actually written down. By watching a certain cake or tea bread being prepared time and time again, a child would soon learn just how much of each ingredient to add to get the perfect result, and would learn to cook from intuition and experience. To a lesser degree, the same thing happens today. Simple cakes and biscuits will be the first experience that many people will have of cookery. They too will have favourite recipes so familiar that they barely need to look at the method or check the measurements. Such familiarity can sometimes be limiting, with people sticking with what they know, and only rarely experimenting with new recipes and unfamiliar techniques.

The choice of recipes in this book covers a broad cross-section of the many branches of baking, and includes recipes for sponge cakes, tea breads and yeast cakes, as well as tarts and pastries. Some of the recipes, particularly the recipes for biscuits, are quick and easy to prepare, and act as the perfect introduction for the novice cook. Others, like the yeast breads, are more complicated and are suitable for the more experienced baker. Hopefully the recipes, which include specialities from other countries, will give you some new ideas and increase your range of skills. The step-by-step format highlights some of the techniques involved and helps you to avoid some of the most common pitfalls.

Baking can be cookery at its most creative and, with the advent of electric mixers, food processors and blenders, it no longer needs to be time consuming. Basic techniques used in baking can now be carried out in a fraction of the time and, with the important exception of pastry, with excellent results. So it is possible for you to make delicious cakes and pastries to delight your friends and family, without necessarily spending hours in the kitchen.

Apple Tart

MAKES 1 TART

The rich pastry in this tart makes it particularly special.

PREPARATION: 30 mins
COOKING: 35-40 mins

Pastry
180g/6oz self-raising flour
Salt
3 tbsps sugar
Dash vanilla essence or 5ml/1tsp grated lemon
   rind
150g/5oz butter or margarine
2 egg yolks or 1 whole egg
1-2 tbsps milk or water

Filling
450g/1lb dessert apples
Sugar for dredging

1. Sift the flour, salt and sugar into a large bowl. Rub in the fat until the mixture resembles fine breadcrumbs.

Step 1 Rub the butter into the dry ingredients until the mixture resembles fine breadcrumbs.

Step 3 Press the pastry into the flan dish, making sure the base and sides are of even thickness. Trim off any excess pastry.

2. Make a well in the centre and place in the egg yolks or the whole egg. Add the vanilla or lemon rind and 1 tbsp milk or water. Mix into the flour with a fork. If the pastry appears too dry, add the additional milk or water.

3. Knead together quickly to smooth out. If the mixture is too soft, wrap well and chill briefly.

4. Press the pastry on the base and up the sides of a flan dish and chill 15 minutes.

5. Meanwhile, prepare the fruit. Peel, core and quarter the apples and slice thinly. Arrange the apple on the base of the flan in circles with the slices slightly overlapping. Sprinkle on sugar and bake in a preheated oven at 200°C/400°F/ Gas Mark 6 until the pastry is pale golden brown and the fruit is soft. Allow to cool before serving.

Royal Mazurek

SERVES 8

The pastry for this traditional Polish cake needs careful handling.

PREPARATION: 30 mins, plus 1 hr to chill the
    pastry
COOKING: 20-30 mins

180g/6oz butter or margarine
60g/2oz sugar
90g/3oz blanched almonds, finely chopped
½ tsp grated lemon rind
300g/10oz plain flour
Yolks of 2 hard-boiled eggs, sieved
1 raw egg yolk
Pinch salt
Pinch cinnamon
Apricot, raspberry or cherry preserves
Icing sugar

1. Cream the butter and the sugar together until light and fluffy. Stir in the almonds, lemon rind, flour and egg yolks by hand. Add the raw egg yolk, a pinch of salt and cinnamon, and mix into a smooth dough. Wrap well and leave in the refrigerator for about 1 hour.

2. Roll out ⅔ of the dough and place on a baking sheet. If dough cracks, press back into

Step 3 Arrange the strips in a latticework pattern on top of the pastry base, pressing edges together well.

place. Meanwhile keep remaining dough in the refrigerator.

3. Roll out the remaining dough and cut into strips about 5mm/¼ inch thick. Arrange these strips on top of the dough in a lattice pattern and press the edges to seal.

4. Brush the pastry with a little beaten egg. Bake in a preheated oven 190°C/375°F/Gas Mark 5 for about 20-30 minutes, or until light golden brown and crisp. Loosen the pastry from the baking sheet but do not remove until completely cool. Place the pastry on a serving plate and spoon some preserve into each of the open spaces of the lattice work. Sprinkle lightly with icing sugar before serving.

Almond Cookies

MAKES 30

When making these cookies, do not overbeat the mixture once the almonds are added, as it will become too sticky to shape.

PREPARATION: 10 mins
COOKING: 12-15 minutes per batch

120g/4oz butter or margarine
60g/2oz caster sugar
30g/1oz light brown sugar
1 egg, beaten
Almond essence
120g/4oz plain flour
1 tsp baking powder
Pinch salt
30g/1oz ground almonds
2 tbsps water
30 whole blanched almonds

1. Cream the butter or margarine together with the two sugars until light and fluffy.

Step 2 Add egg and flavouring and beat until smooth.

Step 3 Shape into small balls with floured hands on a floured surface. Place well apart on baking sheets.

2. Divide the beaten egg in half and add half to the sugar mixture with a few drops of the almond essence and beat until smooth. Reserve the remaining egg for later use. Sift the flour, baking powder and salt into the egg mixture and add the ground almonds. Stir well by hand.

3. Shape the mixture into small balls and place well apart on a lightly greased baking sheet. Flatten slightly and press an almond on to the top of each one.

4. Mix the reserved egg with the water and brush each cookie before baking.

5. Place in a preheated 180°C/350°F/Gas Mark 4 oven and bake for 12-15 minutes. Cookies will be a pale golden colour when done.

Spiced Biscuits

MAKES 15

Crunchy and wholesome, these spicy biscuits are a tea-time treat.

PREPARATION: 20 mins
COOKING: 15 mins

120g/4oz wholewheat flour
½ tsp bicarbonate of soda
1 tsp ground cinnamon
1 tsp ground mixed spice
60g/2oz rolled oats
90g/3oz soft brown sugar
90g/3oz butter
1 tbsp golden syrup
1 tbsp milk

1. Put the flour, bicarbonate of soda, cinnamon, mixed spice, oats and sugar into a bowl and stir well.

Step 3 Pour the melted mixture into the dry ingredients and mix thoroughly to form a pliable dough.

Step 5 Flatten each ball of dough slightly with the back of a wetted spoon.

2. In a saucepan, melt the butter with the syrup and milk over a gentle heat.

3. Pour the melted mixture into the dry ingredients and beat well, until the mixture forms a pliable dough.

4. Divide the mixture into about 15 small balls. Place these onto lightly greased baking sheets, keeping them well spaced, to allow the mixture to spread.

5. Flatten each ball with the back of a wetted spoon, and bake in a preheated oven, 180°C/350°F/Gas Mark 4, for 15 minutes, or until golden brown.

6. Allow the biscuits to cool on the baking sheet before removing them.

Strawberry Shortcake

SERVES 6

These delicious scone-like cakes can be made in advance.

PREPARATION: 30-35 mins
COOKING: 15 mins

225g/8oz plain flour
1 tbsp baking powder
Pinch salt
45g/1½oz sugar
90g/3oz cream cheese, softened
45g/1½oz butter or margarine
1 egg, beaten
90-120ml/3-4 fl oz milk
Melted butter
450g/1lb fresh or frozen strawberries
Juice of half an orange
280ml/½ pint whipped cream

1. Sift the flour, baking powder, salt and sugar into a large bowl.

2. Cut in the cheese and butter or margarine.

3. Blend in the egg and enough milk to make a firm dough.

4. Knead lightly on a floured surface and then roll out to a thickness of 1.25cm/½ inch.

5. Cut the dough into an even number of circles. Re-roll the trimmings and cut as before.

Step 5 Brush one half of the dough circles with butter and place the other halves on top, pressing down lightly.

Brush half of the circles with the melted butter and place the other halves on top, pressing down lightly. Bake on an ungreased baking sheet for about 15 minutes in a pre-heated 225°C/425°F/Gas Mark 7 oven. Allow to cool slightly and then transfer to a wire rack.

6. Hull the strawberries and wash well. Purée half of them with the orange juice. Cut the remaining strawberries in half and combine with the purée.

7. Separate the shortcakes in half and place the bottoms on serving plates. Spoon over the strawberry sauce and the cream.

8. Place the tops of the shortcake on top of the cream.

Carrot Cake

MAKES 1 LOAF

Carrots have long been used as a sweet ingredient, and this cake is moist and absolutely delicious.

PREPARATION: 30 mins
COOKING: 45-50 mins

180g/6oz butter
180g/6oz soft brown sugar
2 eggs, beaten
225g/8oz plain flour
1½ tsps bicarbonate of soda
½ tsp baking powder
½ tsp ground cinnamon
¼ tsp cardamom seeds, crushed
225g/8oz peeled carrots, grated
90g/3oz raisins
60g/2oz walnuts, chopped
2 tbsps clear honey
Icing sugar, for dredging

1. Cream the butter and sugar together, until they are light and fluffy.

Step 1 Cream the margarine and sugar together, until they are light and fluffy.

Step 3 Fold the dry ingredients carefully, but thoroughly, into the egg mixture, using a metal spoon.

2. Add the eggs, a little at a time, beating well after each addition.

3. Mix the flour with the bicarbonate of soda, baking powder, cinnamon and cardamom and fold into the egg mixture.

4. Stir in the carrots, raisins and nuts, along with the honey. Mix well, to blend thoroughly.

5. Pour the mixture into a well-buttered 25cm/10-inch loaf tin. Bake in a preheated oven, 180°C/350°F/Gas Mark 4, for 45-50 minutes, or until a fine metal skewer comes out clean, when inserted into the centre of the cake.

6. Cool the cake in the tin for 10-15 minutes, before turning out carefully onto a wire rack, to cool completely.

7. Dredge the cake with icing sugar before serving.

Spiced Cranberry Nut Tea Bread

MAKES 1 LOAF

Tea breads don't rely on yeast to make them rise so they are quick and easy to prepare.

PREPARATION: 25 mins
COOKING: 1 hr

225g/8oz plain flour
1 tsp baking powder
225g/8oz sugar
1 tsp baking soda
Pinch salt
¼ tsp ground nutmeg
¼ tsp ground ginger
4 fl oz orange juice
30g/1oz butter, melted
60ml/4 tbsps water
1 egg, beaten
120g/4oz fresh cranberries, roughly chopped
120g/4oz hazelnuts, roughly chopped

1. Sift the dry ingredients and spices into a large mixing bowl. Pour in the orange juice, melted butter, water and egg and beat the mixture with a wooden spoon.

2. Add the cranberries and nuts and stir to mix.

Step 1 Pour in the liquid ingredients and gradually incorporate the flour from the outside edge.

3. Lightly grease a loaf tin about 22 × 12.5cm/ 9" × 5". Press a strip of greaseproof paper on the base and up the sides. Lightly grease the paper and flour the whole inside of the pan. Spoon in the bread mixture and bake in a pre-heated 170°C/325°F/Gas Mark 3 oven for about 1 hour, or until a skewer inserted into the centre of the loaf comes out clean.

4. Remove from the pan, carefully peel off the paper and cool on a wire rack. Lightly dust with icing sugar and cut into slices to serve.

Gingerbread

MAKES ONE

Dark treacle and fresh ginger combine to make this favourite family cake.

PREPARATION: 15 mins
COOKING: 1-1½ hrs

120g/4oz butter
120g/4 fl oz black treacle
225g/8oz light soft brown sugar
120ml/4 fl oz hot water
300g/10oz plain flour
2 tsps baking powder
2 tsps fresh ginger, peeled and grated
1 tsp grated nutmeg
1 egg, beaten

1. Put the butter, treacle and sugar into a large saucepan. Heat gently, stirring all the time, until the sugar and butter have melted together.

Step 1 Melt the butter, treacle and sugar together in a large saucepan.

Step 6 The cake is done when a skewer inserted into the centre comes out clean.

2. Pour in the hot water, mix well and set aside.

3. Sift the flour with baking powder into a large bowl. Add the ginger, nutmeg and beaten egg.

4. Gradually beat in the treacle mixture, using a wooden spoon and drawing the flour from the outside into the centre.

5. Line the base of a 7-inch square cake tin with lightly greased greaseproof paper.

6. Pour the gingerbread mixture into the cake tin, and bake in a preheated oven 160°C/325°F/Gas Mark 3, for 1-1½ hours, testing during this time with a skewer; which should come out clean when the cake is cooked.

7. Allow the cake to cool in the tin, before turning out onto a wire rack.

Poppy Seed Cake

MAKES 2 ROLLS

A Christmas version of an ever popular Polish cake.

PREPARATION: 1 hr
COOKING: 45-50 mins

Pastry Dough
675g/1½lbs flour
180g/6oz sugar
180g/6oz butter or margarine
2 eggs
90-120ml/3-4 fl oz milk
45g/3 tbsps yeast

Filling
225g/8oz poppy seeds
430ml/¾ pint milk
90g/3oz butter or margarine
140ml/¼ pint honey
60g/2oz ground walnuts
90g/3oz raisins
30g/1oz finely chopped glacé peel
2 eggs
120g/4oz sugar
90ml/3 fl oz brandy

1. To make the dough, cream the butter and sugar, then gradually add the eggs, beating between each addition. Heat the milk until lukewarm, dissolve the yeast in it and add to the other ingredients. Sift in the flour and a pinch of salt and knead well.

2. Knead the dough on a lightly-floured surface, stretching it well. When the dough

Step 5 Roll up the dough as for a swiss roll.

springs back fairly quickly to the touch place it in a lightly greased bowl, cover and leave for 1 hour in a warm place to rise.

3. Boil milk for filling and add poppy seeds. Cook gently for 30 minutes, stirring often. Drain the seeds and blend to a paste.

4. Melt the butter and add honey, walnuts, raisins and peel. Add the poppy seed and cook gently for 15 minutes, stirring well. Beat the eggs and sugar, then combine with the poppy seed mixture. Cook slowly stirring constantly to thicken. Add the brandy then set aside.

5. When the dough has doubled in bulk, knock it back and knead for a few minutes. Divide dough in half. Roll each half out thinly on a floured surface. Spread the filling evenly over each piece, roll up as for a swiss roll and press the ends together. Place on a greased baking sheet. Bake at 190°C/375°F/Gas Mark 5 for 45-50 minutes.

Saffron Babas

MAKES 2 CAKES

A light textured yeast cake.

PREPARATION: 2 hrs
COOKING: 1 hr

300g/10oz plain flour
430ml/¾ pint lukewarm milk
90g/3oz yeast
180g/6oz sugar
8 egg yolks
4 egg whites
Rind of 1 lemon
45ml/3 tbsps brandy
Pinch saffron powder
900g/2lbs plain flour
Pinch salt
180g/6oz melted butter, slightly cooled
120g/4oz sultanas
30g/1oz mixed peel

1. Sift 300g/10oz flour into a large mixing bowl. Combine the milk and yeast and pour into the flour. Mix well with a wooden spoon.

2. Cover the batter and leave in a warm place for 1 hour, until it doubles in bulk and the top becomes bubbly.

3. Combine the sugar together with the egg yolks, egg whites, lemon rind, brandy and saffron. Mix with the yeast mixture and add the

Step 2 Leave in a warm place until doubled in bulk and bubbly on top.

remaining flour and salt. Knead the dough by hand for about 30 minutes on a well-floured surface.

4. Place the dough back in the bowl and add the butter, raisins and peel. Knead until it is smooth and elastic. Divide in 2 equal portions. Butter 2 25cm/10 inch round cake pans very thickly and place in the dough, patting out evenly. Cover and put in a warm place to rise until it fills the pan. Bake in a pre-heated 200°C/400°F/Gas Mark 7 oven for about 1 hour.

5. Test with a metal skewer. If the skewer comes out clean when inserted into the centre of the babas the cakes are done. Leave to cool in the pans for about 10-14 mintues and then remove to a cooling rack. Sprinkle with sugar or drizzel with icing.

Chocolate Cinnamon Bread

MAKES 1 LOAF

Pull this bread apart to serve in individual pieces rather than slicing it.

PREPARATION: 2 hrs
COOKING: 45-50 mins

Dough
4 tbsps warm water
½oz sugar
1 envelope dry yeast
340-400g/12-14oz strong flour
90g/3oz sugar
Pinch salt
75g/2½oz butter, softened
5 eggs, beaten

Topping
120g/4oz butter, melted
225g/8oz sugar
2 tsps cinnamon
2 tsps cocoa
90g/6 tbsps finely chopped nuts

---

1. Sprinkle ½oz sugar and the yeast on top of the water and leave it in a warm place until foaming.

2. Sift 340g/12oz of flour into a bowl and add the sugar and salt. Rub in the butter until completely blended.

3. Add 2 eggs and the yeast mixture, mixing in well. Add the remaining eggs one at a time until the mixture forms a soft, spongy dough. Add

Step 5 Roll the dough in melted butter and then in the sugar mixture.

remaining flour as necessary. Knead for 10 minutes on a lightly floured surface until smooth.

4. Place the dough in a greased bowl, cover loosely and put in a warm place. Leave to stand for 1-1½ hours or until doubled in bulk.

5. Butter a ring mould liberally. Knock the dough down and knead it again for about 5 minutes. Shape into balls about 5cm/2 inches in diameter. Mix the topping ingredients together except for the melted butter. Roll the dough balls in the butter and then in the sugar mixture.

6. Place the dough balls in the bottom of the mould. Cover and allow to rise again about 15 minutes. Bake in a pre-heated 180°C/350°F/ Gas Mark 4 oven for about 45-50 minutes. Loosen from the pan and turn out while still warm.

Lemon and Raisin Tea Cakes

MAKES ABOUT 24

*Cooked rice is the surprise ingredient in these cakes that are crisp outside,
yet soft and light inside.*

PREPARATION: 40 mins
COOKING: 40-45 mins

120g/4oz long-grain rice, cooked
120g/4oz plain flour
1 tsp baking powder
Pinch salt
120g/4oz sugar
2 eggs, separated
90ml/6 tbsps milk
Grated rind of 1 lemon
60g/2oz raisins

1. Cook the rice, rinse, drain and leave to cool.

2. Sift the flour, baking powder and salt into a mixing bowl and stir in the sugar.

3. Beat the yolks with the milk and add

Step 4 Mix a spoonful of whites into the rice mixture to lighten it. Fold in the remaining whites using a large spoon.

Step 5 Drop the mixture by spoonfuls into a hot frying pan. Cook until brown on both sides.

gradually to the dry ingredients, stirring constantly, to make a thick batter. Stir in the rice.

4. Beat the egg whites until stiff but not dry and fold into the batter along with the lemon rind and raisins.

5. Lightly oil the base of a heavy frying pan and place over moderate heat. When the pan is hot, drop in about 15ml/1 tbsp of batter and if necessary, spread into a small circle with the back of the spoon.

6. Cook until brown on one side and bubbles form on the top surface. Turn over and cook the other side. Cook 4-6 at a time.

7. Repeat until all the batter is used, keeping the cakes warm. Serve plain or buttered.

Corn Meal Muffins

MAKES 12

These muffins are slightly sweet and crumbly.

PREPARATION: 20 mins
COOKING: 14 mins

120g/4oz plain flour
60g/2oz sugar
2 tsps baking powder
½ tsp salt
150g/5oz yellow cornmeal
1 egg, beaten
4 tbsps oil
370ml/11 fl oz milk

1. Pre-heat the oven to 250°C/450°F/Gas Mark 8. Grease a 12-space patty tin liberally with oil. Heat the pans for 5 minutes in the oven.

Step 5 Spoon the batter into the prepared pans. It may be slightly lumpy.

Step 2 Sift the dry ingredients into a large bowl, leaving a well in the centre.

2. Sift the flour, sugar, baking powder and salt into a large bowl. Add the cornmeal and stir to blend, leaving a well in the centre.

3. Combine the egg, oil and milk and pour into the well.

4. Beat with a wooden spoon, gradually incorporating the dry ingredients into the liquid. Do not overbeat the mixture. It can be slightly lumpy.

5. Spoon the batter into the pans and bake for about 14 minutes.

6. Cool briefly in the pans and then remove to a wire rack to cool further. Serve warm.

Pecan Pastries

MAKES 12

These sweet, nutty pastries are deep-fried to make them light and crisp.

PREPARATION: 30 mins
COOKING: 2 mins

120g/4oz plain flour
1 tsp baking powder
¼ tsp salt
4 tbsps cold water
Oil for frying
280ml/½ pint golden syrup mixed with
    140ml/¼ pint treacle
90g/3oz finely chopped pecans

---

1. Sift the flour, baking powder and salt together in a large bowl. Make a well in the centre and pour in the cold water.

Step 1 Sift the dry ingredients into a bowl and make a well in the centre.

Step 3 On a floured surface, roll out each piece until very thin.

2. Mix until a stiff dough forms, and then knead by hand until smooth.

3. Divide the dough into 12 portions, each about the size of a walnut. Roll out each portion of dough on a floured surface until very thin.

4. Heat the oil in a deep fat fryer to 180°C/350°F. Drop each piece of pastry into the hot fat using two forks. Twist the pastry just as it hits the oil. Cook one at a time until light brown.

5. In a large saucepan, boil the syrup until it forms a soft ball when dropped into cold water.

6. Drain the pastries on paper towels after frying and dip carefully into the hot syrup. Sprinkle with pecans before the syrup sets and allow to cool before serving.

Flourless Chocolate Cake

SERVES 6

This soufflé cake is adored by chocolate lovers everywhere.

PREPARATION: 15 minutes
COOKING: 1 hr 15 mins

450g/1lb plain chocolate
30ml/2 tbsps strong coffee
30ml/2 tbsps brandy
6 eggs
90g/3oz sugar
280ml/½ pint whipping cream
Icing sugar
Fresh whole strawberries

Step 5 Pour the cake mixture into the prepared pan and then place it in a bain marie.

1. Melt the chocolate in the top of a double boiler. Stir in the coffee and brandy and leave to cool slightly.

2. Break up the eggs and then, using an electric mixer, gradually beat in the sugar until the mixture is thick. When the beaters are lifted the mixture should mound slightly.

3. Whip the cream until soft peaks form.

4. Beat the chocolate, and gradually add the egg mixture to it.

5. Fold in the cream and pour the cake mixture into a well greased deep 22cm/9" cake pan with a disk of greaseproof paper in the bottom.

Bake in a pre-heated 180°C/350°F/Gas Mark 5 oven in a bain marie. To make a bain marie, use a roasting pan and fill with warm water to come halfway up the side of the cake pan.

6. Bake about 1 hour and then turn off the oven, leaving the cake inside to stand for 15 minutes. Loosen the sides of the cake carefully from the pan and allow the cake to cool completely before turning it out.

7. Invert the cake onto a serving plate and carefully peel off the paper. Place strips of greaseproof paper on top of the cake, leaving even spaces in between the strips. Sprinkle the top with icing sugar and carefully lift off the paper strips. Decorate with whole strawberries.

Almond Torte

MAKES 1 CAKE

Whipped egg whites make this cake light and fluffy.

PREPARATION: 30 mins
COOKING: 30-40 mins

60g/2oz dry breadcrumbs
120ml/4 fl oz milk
1 tbsp rum
90g/3oz butter or margarine
90g/3oz sugar
6 eggs, separated
90g/3oz ground roasted almonds
570ml/1 pint double cream
30g/1oz sugar
15ml/1 tbsp rum
60g/2oz roasted almonds, finely chopped
Whole blanched almonds, toasted

---

1. Preheat the oven to 180°C/350°F/Gas Mark 4. Soak the breadcrumbs in milk and rum in a large bowl.

Step 2 Fold the egg whites into the crumb mixture along with the almonds using a large spoon or a rubber spatula.

Step 4
Sandwich the layers of cake together with the almond cream.

2. In a separate bowl, cream the butter and sugar until light and fluffy. Beat in the egg yolks one at a time and then add to the crumb mixture. Beat the egg whites until stiff and fold into the crumb mixture along with the almonds.

3. Grease and flour three 20cm/8 inch round cake pans. Divide the cake mixture among the pans and bake for 30-40 minutes. Allow to cool briefly in the pans, loosen the sides and remove the cakes to a rack to finish cooling.

4. Whip the cream and the sugar with the rum. Reserve one third of the cream for the top and fold the finely chopped almonds into the remaining two thirds. Sandwich the cake layers together with the almond cream and spread a layer of plain cream on top, reserving some for piping.

5. Pipe out rosettes with the remaining cream on top of the cake. Decorate with the whole almonds.

Cinnamon Buttercream Cake

MAKES 1 CAKE

A cake that doesn't need baking is convenient any time, and perfect for summer.

PREPARATION: 45 mins

280g/10oz sugar
1 cinnamon stick
90ml/6 tbsps water
8 egg yolks
450g/1lb unsalted butter, softened
24 sponge fingers
90ml/6 tbsps brandy
90g/3oz toasted almonds, roughly chopped
90g/3oz plain chocolate, coarsely grated

1. Put the sugar, water and cinnamon stick in a small, heavy-based saucepan and bring to the boil, stirring until the sugar dissolves.

2. Allow to boil briskly without stirring until the syrup reaches a temperature of 113°C/236°F on a sugar thermometer.

3. While the sugar syrup is boiling, beat the egg yolks in a large bowl until they are thick. Soften the butter until light and fluffy.

4. When the syrup is ready, quickly pour it in a thin, steady stream into the egg yolks, beating constantly.

5. Continue beating until the mixture is thick and creamy. Allow to cool.

6. Beat in the softened butter, a spoonful at a time. Chill the mixture until it is of spreading consistency.

Step 4 Pour the prepared syrup in a thin, steady stream onto the egg yolks while beating with an electric whisk.

7. Cut the sponge fingers to fit closely together in a 20cm/8 inch square pan. Line the pan with lightly greased foil or paper.

8. Spread some of the buttercream lightly on one side of the biscuits and place them, icing side down, in the pan. Cut small pieces of biscuits to fill in any corners, if necessary.

9. Sprinkle over half of the brandy. Spread over another layer of buttercream and place on the remaining biscuits. Sprinkle over the remaining brandy and cover the top with buttercream, reserving some for the sides. Place the cake in the refrigerator and chill until firm.

10. When the icing is firm, remove the cake from the refrigerator and lift it out of the pan using the foil or paper. Slide onto a flat surface and spread the sides with the remaining buttercream. Press the almonds into the sides and decorate the top with grated chocolate.

Guinness Cake

MAKES 1 CAKE

This dark, moist fruit cake makes an ideal Christmas, or rich birthday cake.

PREPARATION: 20 mins
COOKING: 2 hrs

225g/8oz margarine
180g/6oz soft brown sugar
280ml/½ pint Guinness, or stout
225g/8oz raisins
225g/8oz currants
225g/8oz sultanas
120g/4oz chopped mixed peel
560g/1¼ lbs wholemeal plain flour
1 tsp mixed spice
1 tsp nutmeg
½ tsp bicarbonate of soda
3 eggs, beaten

1. Grease and line a 23cm/9-inch cake tin with greaseproof paper.

2. Put the margarine, sugar and Guinness into

Step 1 Line the base and the sides of the greased cake tin with greaseproof paper, making sure that it fits well into the corners.

Step 3 Simmer the dried fruit and peel in the sugar and Guinness mixture for 5 minutes.

a large saucepan and bring the ingredients slowly to the boil, stirring all the time, until the sugar and the margarine have melted.

3. Stir the dried fruit and peel into the Guinness mixture, and bring all the ingredients back to the boil. Simmer for 5 minutes. Remove from the heat and leave, until the mixture is quite cold.

4. Put the flour, spices and bicarbonate of soda into a large mixing bowl.

5. Beat the cooled fruit mixture and the eggs into the flour, mixing well with a wooden spoon, to ensure that the flour is thoroughly incorporated and there are no lumps.

6. Pour the cake mixture into the prepared tin, and bake in the centre of a preheated oven, 160°C/325°F/Gas Mark 3, for 2 hours.

7. Cool the cake in the tin, before turning it out.

Index

Pecan Pastries are both sweet and nutty.